T!

MESSI/

The astounding discovery of the identity and mission of Israel's Messiah revealed in the ancient Hebrew names, Genealogies, Pictographs and types found in the Hebrew Scriptures of the Old Testament, the Tenach.

All bible quotations are taken from the 1611 King James Holy Bible

The Messiah Code

Copyright

Bob Mitchell

2014

THE MESSIAH CODE

THE MESSIAH CODE

Introduction

The bible is the most incredible document on the face of the earth. However the last 150 years has witnessed concerted attacks on the Holy bible's reliability; textually, historically, prophetically and spiritually like no other book.

For those who led the attack this has resulted in an unmitigated defeat in all areas. While the discovery of the Dead Sea Scrolls between 1947 and the early 1950's settled forever the historical and textual reliability of ancient scripture, the attacks against it being the inspired word of God; a message from beyond this physical world regarding earth's origin, the entry of sin and the promise of a redeemer, the Messiah, who would die for the sins of the world, have continued unabated.

Many Jewish people, whose ancestors were the God ordained guardians of the scriptures, deny any suggestion that Jesus Christ was the longed for promised one. They deny the Messiah would die for the redemption from sin. In their eyes the Messiah will be one who would rescue them from their oppressors and establish the kingdom of God on earth. Jesus (Yeshua), they say, did not do this.

They disregard their own scriptures such as Psalm 22, Isaiah 53, Daniel 9 and others that foretell the suffering servant, the Messiah who would die for the sins of the world. To many these scriptures are a picture, not of a coming Messiah who would die for their sins and return later to establish the physical Kingdom of God, but of the continual suffering of the Jewish people.

I have felt for many years if God really is God almighty then when he inspired the ancient scriptures he must have known the Jewish people would later reject their own Messiah. Therefore, I reasoned, there must be a way God, in his wisdom, provided another way, another source contained within his word that would show Jesus was / is the Jewish

Messiah and Saviour of the world; a source that has its roots firmly based within ancient Judaism.

Yet at the same time the hidden message must be placed there not only under divine guidance but be a message contrary to that accepted by the Jewish people and their religious leaders even though it was placed there unknowingly by their ancestors.

This is the story of Jesus revealed in the Hebrew bible as Messiah, but without using the ancient prophecies one usually enlists as evidence.

Instead on our adventure we shall journey beneath the ancient Hebrew text to discover what I have called THE MESSIAH CODE; An ancient Hebrew code Millennia old and accessible to any who desire to know the truth regarding the identity of the Messiah.

Please Note: I shall be using the names *Jesus* and *Yeshua* but they both refer to the same person. *Yeshua* is *Jesus'* Hebrew name. The name *Jesus* is the English version of the Greek transliteration of the Hebrew name *Yeshua* so please do not be confused *Yeshua* and *Jesus* refer to the same person.

Chapter 1

IS JESUS THE PROMISED MESSIAH?

Although Christians attempt to prove Jesus is the Messiah by the messianic prophecies in the Old Testament, for many that simply is not enough.

Is there another way to present evidence for the Messiahship of the Lord Jesus?

The Messiah himself said in John 5:39: *Search the scriptures; for in them ye think ye have eternal life: and they are they which testify of me.*

But which scriptures? On resurrection morning two despondent, rejected and frightened disciples were hurriedly leaving Jerusalem and possible persecution and even arrest and execution for being followers of the man from Galilee who had been executed for blasphemy and claiming to be the king of the Jews.

As they walked along the dusty road to Emmaus, just 12 miles away, the resurrected Jesus appeared and caught up with them as if he were another traveller. After asking them concerning their sad appearance and recent events in the city they explained to him their bitter disappointment that the one on whom they had placed their hopes was now dead and buried.

With almost heartbreaking love and tenderness the risen Messiah spoke to them: *Then he said unto them, O fools, and slow of heart to believe all that the prophets have spoken: Ought not Christ to have suffered these things, and to enter into his glory? And beginning at Moses and all the prophets, he expounded unto them in all the scriptures the things concerning himself.* Luke 24:25, 26.

This scripture captured my imagination. If I could find just some of the scriptures that would prove Jesus (Yeshua) is without doubt the Messiah how wonderful it would be. There are scriptures in the surface text of the Old Testament that point to the coming one yet they are interpreted in a different way by many Jewish scholars and Rabbis today. What if God had placed within the text evidence that could only be denied by the most hard headed sceptic?

If only I could find a few...just a few.....

When the book "The Bible Code" was first published in 1995 I was excited with the prospect that these codes might reveal Jesus as Messiah. I was disappointed to say the least. In fact there were no Messiah codes at all. Later Grant Jeffrey and Yacov Rambsell were said to have discovered codes that revealed the identity of the coming one as Jesus. But these were codes with a name, a place etc. but no actual message. Still I was not completely satisfied. I wanted more.

It was then I made some astonishing discoveries.

Chapter 2

ADAM TO NOAH

First some hardy researchers had discovered when one changed the names of Adam and his descendents into the root Hebrew meaning of their names a stunning message is revealed.

ADAM'S FAMILY TREE AND THE GOSPEL MESSAGE

Adam's name means man. Following the murder of her son Abel by his brother Cain, Adam's wife Eve gave birth to another son, Seth. She said God had appointed her another son. The Hebrew name Seth means "Appointed". Seth had a son named Enosh. Enosh means "Mortal". Enosh had a son named Kenan meaning "Sorrow". And so the list continues. Kenan's son Mahalalel means "The Blessed God". Jared, Mahalalel's son means "He Who Descends". Next came Enoch. Enoch was a teacher of righteousness, therefore many Christian preachers believe his name means "Teaching". But my research through Jewish sources reveals the name to mean "Dedicated". Next in the genealogy is Methuselah whose name means "His Death Shall Bring". This is very interesting because a study of the births and deaths of the descendants of Adam shows us the very year Methuselah died at the ripe old age of 969 was the same year the flood of Noah came. When Methuselah died the flood came. His death brought on the flood. Methuselah's son Lamech was the father of Noah and Lamech translates as "Despairing". Noah is the last in the genealogy of Genesis 5. His name means "Comfort or Rest".

(Fig1)

NAME	MEANING
ADAM	███
SETH	███
ENOSH	███
KENAN	███
MAHALALEL	███
JARED	███
ENOCH	███
• METHUSELAH	███
LAMECH	███
NOAH	███

When I read the list of names in their root Hebrew form the message almost blew my mind.

(Fig 2)

NAME	MEANING
ADAM	MAN
SETH	APPOINTED
ENOSH	MORTAL
KENAN	SORROW
MAHALALEL	THE BLESSED GOD
JARED	HE WHO DESCENDS
ENOCH	IS DEDICATED
METHUSELAH	HIS DEATH SHALL BRING
LAMECH	THE DESPAIRING
NOAH	COMFORT, REST

MAN APPOINTED MORTAL SORROW. THE BLESSED GOD, HE WHO DESCENDS, IS DEDICATED. HIS DEATH SHALL BRING THE DESPAIRING COMFORT AND REST.

This is the Gospel in Genesis the first book of the bible! That is simply taking each name from the genealogy of Adam to Noah as recorded in Genesis 5 and taking the name back to the original root meaning in Hebrew. How could, why would, a Jewish scribe writing this down present to us the astounding message that God himself would come to earth and die giving lost men rest and comfort because of the forgiveness of sins he brings?

The simple answer is he couldn't. But an unseen hand controls history even the genealogy and the very names of our first parents and their descendants. It is the hand of God Himself.

Now to the second discovery I made. In the Hebrew language every letter has a number, a colour, a picture and even a musical note as we show in the DVD "Jesus in the Old Testament".

I began to wonder about the Hebrew pictographs. The pictographs can be dated back many thousands of years even before the time of Christ. Each picture tells a part of a story or message; I believe it is a message from eternity to those who are willing to listen and believe.

Chapter 3

BERESHIT

(Fig 3)

HEBREW PICTOGRAPHS

Name	Pictograph	Meaning	Name	Pictograph	Meaning
Aleph		Ox / strength / leader	Lamed		Staff / goad / control / "toward"
Bet		House / "In"	Mem		Water / chaos
Gimmel		Foot / camel / pride	Nun		Seed / fish / activity / life
Dalet		Tent door / pathway	Samekh		Hand on staff / support / prop
Hey		Lo! Behold! "The"	Ayin		Eye / to see / experience
Vav		Nail / peg / add / "And"	Pey		Mouth / word / speak
Zayin		Plow / weapon / cut off	Tsade		Man on side / desire / need
Chet		Tent wall / fence / separation	Qof		Sun on horizon / behind
Tet		Basket / snake / surround	Resh		Head / person / first
Yod		Arm and hand / work / deed	Shin		Eat / consume / destroy
Kaf		Palm of hand / to open	Tav		Mark / sign / covenant

The above illustration is a generalisation of the meanings of each letter. For instance Aleph can also mean sacrifice as it is in the shape of an ox and oxen were used in the sacrifices of Israel. Or it can mean God as the first above all. Tav is the last letter of the Hebrew "Aleph-bet" and like Aleph and many of the other letters can simply mean cross because of its shape.

Again I wondered is there a message here somewhere? I began my search in the very first word of the Old Testament "Bereshit" meaning "In the beginning." What would happen if I took the ancient pictographs and substituted them for the Hebrew letters in Bereshit? Would there be a message hidden beneath the surface text?

I was not disappointed.

Jesus (Yeshua) when debating with his fellow countrymen, the Jews, said in John chapter 2 verse 19 "Destroy this temple and in three days I will raise it up". Of course he was speaking of his own body being a temple in which the Holy Spirit dwelt. The Shekinah; the very presence of God himself was dwelling inside the body of Yeshua. He is the one who existed before time itself began and is the very creator of all things. Just as the very presence of God had once been in residence within the ancient Tabernacle in the wilderness (more on this later) and later within the Holy of Holies of the Temple in Jerusalem, now here standing in human form was God in the flesh and within that body dwelt the Shekinah glory; the living God himself on earth and moving among his people.   Also in chapter 10 verses 17 and 18 of John Jesus stated: "Therefore doth my Father love me, because I lay down my life, that I might take it again. 18 No man taketh it from me, but I lay it down of myself. I have power to lay it down, and I have power to take it again. This commandment have I received of my Father".

In the pictograph of Bereshit, the first word of Genesis 1, we read from right to left:

בּ Beit which is a picture of a house or the temple,   ר Resh meaning the highest,   א Aleph which can mean God or sacrifice,   שׁ Shin meaning to be destroyed or to destroy,   י Yod meaning hand or one's own hand,   ת Tav meaning a cross. (See fig 4)

The stunning message we receive from Genesis 1 in ancient Hebrew Pictographs and Bereshit the very first Hebrew word in the bible is:

The house / temple of the highest sacrifice (or God) will be destroyed by his own hand on a cross.

(Fig 4)

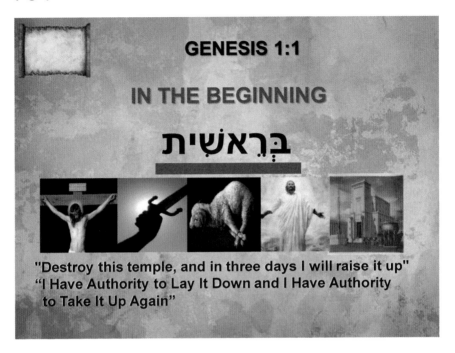

Isn't that incredible? To discover the Gospel message hidden in the first Hebrew word of the bible? Hidden in ancient Hebrew pictographs. All the more stunning when one realises the modern religious Jew does not believe God would come and die on a cross for their sins. Yet here it is revealed in the Hebrew pictographs proving, yet again, God authored the bible; placing within the Hebrew text proof they cannot deny from their own ancient pictographic history. Yeshua is God and came and died on the cross for our sins. The message was placed there by a divine hand at the very beginning of the Hebrew bible thousands of years before crucifixion was ever invented!

CHAPTER 4

ABRAHAM AND ISAAC AND YESHUA

But there is more. Let us take the story of Abraham and Isaac. In Genesis 22 we read the story of God's call to Abraham to sacrifice his own dear son, Isaac. God told Abraham to travel to a certain mountain and there sacrifice Isaac. In complete obedience to God Abraham left his wife Sarah and travelled 3 days until he came to Mount Moriah, today known as the Temple Mount, though today Mount Moriah is split in two halves by the main road that encircles the Old City of Jerusalem. One half contains the Temple Mount while the other continues to the area of the Garden Tomb believed by many to be the original tomb of Yeshua following his crucifixion.

Once they arrived at the foot of Mount Moriah Isaac dutifully gathered the wood for the sacrifice not aware the sacrifice would be him. Abraham told the two servants that had accompanied them to wait and he and the boy would return.

This is a point many miss when reading the account. In saying he and Isaac would return, Abraham revealed his faith in God to an amazing degree. God had previously promised Abraham that he would establish / continue the covenant he had made with Abraham for the land in which they dwelt through Isaac and his descendants. Abraham knew God could not lie so to fulfil his promise he would have to resurrect Isaac if Abraham killed him. Such was the faith of Abraham. May we be granted such faith as he.

But back to the story: Once the wood was prepared, Abraham bound Isaac and laid him on the wood ready to kill his own son in obedience to God's request. But on seeing his faith God sent a ram caught in the thicket and the result was the ram was sacrificed instead.

Now here again is something that many of us read but never stop to ask "why"?

The text says Abraham came down the mountain and returned home with the young men.

WHERE WAS ISAAC? The text simply leaves him out. Why? In fact Isaac is not mentioned for the next two chapters until Abraham's servant brings Rebekah to Isaac, as his bride, from the house of Laban.

Do you see anything here yet?

Let me explain......

(Fig 5 and 6)

THE FATHER RECEIVES THE SON AS FROM THE DEAD.
THE FATHER SENDS THE SERVANT TO FIND A
BRIDE FOR THE SON.
THE SERVANT TAKES GIFTS FOR THE BRIDE
FROM THE FATHER
THE SON IS NOT SEEN AFTER HIS
"RESURRECTION" UNTIL.....
THE SERVANT RETURNS WITH THE BRIDE.
THE NAME OF THE SERVANT IS ELIEZER

ELIEZER MEANS "GOD IS MY HELPER"
THE NAME REBEKAH MEANS "SECURED"
LABAN MEANS WHITE, A REFERENCE TO SIN

TO RECAP:

- THE SON RISES FROM THE DEAD

- THE FATHER SENDS THE SERVANT TO FIND A BRIDE

- THE BRIDE IS "SECURED"

- THE SERVANT GIVES GIFTS TO THE BRIDE FROM THE FATHER

- BUT THE SON IS NOT SEEN AGAIN UNTIL..........

- THE SERVANT RETURNS WITH THE BRIDE FROM

- THE HOUSE OF SIN

Do you see? It is a foretelling of the gospel story.

From the moment God told Abraham to sacrifice his son, Abraham counted Isaac as dead.

For how long? For 3 days. That was the length of the journey to Mount Moriah. Gen. 22:4

For how long was Jesus dead? For 3 days. Luke 24:36

Isaac carried the wood for his own sacrifice to Mount Moriah. Gen. 22:6

Jesus carried the wood for his own sacrifice to Mount Moriah. John 19:17

Abraham received Isaac as if from the dead after the 3 day journey. Heb. 17:19

Jesus rose from the dead after 3 days. Luke 24:36

Isaac was not seen in the text after his "resurrection" Gen. 22:15 - 24:58

Jesus is not seen by the world after his resurrection. John 14:19

Abraham sent his servant to find a bride for Isaac. Gen. 24

The Holy Spirit is sent out to prepare a bride for Jesus. 2 Cor. 11:2

The servant is sent out with gifts for the bride. Gen. 24

The Holy Spirit is sent forth to the bride (church) with spiritual gifts. Acts 2; 1 Cor. 12

Rebekah accepts the gifts and is secured as the bride. Gen. 24

The church is given spiritual gifts as she is betrothed, secured, in Christ. 1 Cor. 12

Isaac isn't seen until the servant brings the bride to him from the house of Laban (sin). Gen. 24

Jesus is not seen until the bride comes out of the world (house of sin) to meet him. 1 Thes.4:16,17

Surely this was not placed in the Old Testament by accident. The whole story of Abram, Isaac and Rebekah, like the rest of Old Testament history is the story of Jesus Christ foretold in the lives of these historical figures.

Chapter 5

THE TWELVE TRIBES

As we move on through the Old Testament we are faced with other amazing evidences of a supernatural authorship from outside of time. A message that transcends the ages with a message of redemption for mankind from a Holy, loving God.

I looked at the list of the 12 tribes the sons of Jacob, Isaac's son. Once again I was stunned with the message I discovered as I dug into the root meaning of the Hebrew names of the founders of the 12 tribes of Israel.

Fig 7

THE TWELVE TRIBES

Reuben -	Behold a son
Simeon -	Hear Him (and)
Levi -	Be Joined
Judah -	Give Him Praise
Dan –	Judge (his)
Naphtali -	Strife (and his)
Gad -	Fortune
Asher -	Happy and Blessed (am I)
Issachar -	He Brings Reward
Zebulun -	Dwelling With Us
Joseph -	He Shall Add(for he is)
Benjamin -	The Son of My Right Hand

Once more we are faced with a message modern Judaism refuses to accept; that God had a son we should praise. One who is the son of God's right hand which makes him God's equal because he himself IS also God.

How wonderful of the creator of all things to place such a message within the very names of the 12 tribes of Israel. And in the New Testament book of Revelation, chapter 21, we find these same names, this same message, embedded in the very walls, the very gates of the Holy city of God, placed there for all eternity.

We find the same message only more graphically displayed when we come to the Tabernacle.

Chapter 6

THE MESSIAH IN THE TABERNACLE

It would take a complete volume on its own to record the wonderful way God has pointed the way to the Lord Yeshua and his redemptive work revealed in every item within the Tabernacle in the wilderness.

We will cover just a few here. When one wanted to enter the Tabernacle area you had to enter through just one door. There was no other way. Yeshua himself told his Jewish people: I am the door: by me if any man enter in, he shall be saved, and shall go in and out, and find pasture. John 10:9. He also said: John 14:6 Jesus saith unto him, I am the way, the truth, and the life: no man cometh unto the Father, but by me.

(Fig 5)

John 14:6 Jesus saith unto him, I am the way, the truth, and the life: no man cometh unto the Father, but by me.

THE DOOR

You see, if any man, woman or child wishes to reach God, the only way is through the one and only door, Yeshua. He alone is the way and there is no other. We either believe the son of God or we believe the ecumenical "one size fits all" camp that believes all roads lead to God as long as you are sincere. The bible says different, so we either believe the scriptures or we stop being "Christian hypocrites" leave the church and admit we do not believe the words of Yeshua.

Either he alone is the only way to God as he said or he isn't. You cannot have it both ways; you cannot tell everyone you are a Christian but disbelieve the words of Christ himself.

Once we have entered the one door (Yeshua) we are immediately faced with the altar of sacrifice. This again is a clear picture of the suffering Messiah; a foretelling of his sacrifice for sin.

(Fig 6)

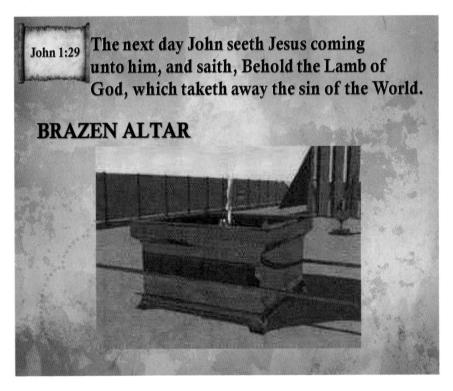

John 1:29 The next day John seeth Jesus coming unto him, and saith, Behold the Lamb of God, which taketh away the sin of the World.

BRAZEN ALTAR

The blood of bulls and goats could never take away sin but they were a deposit, in a sense, looking forward to the one true, final sacrifice for sin when Messiah presented himself as the ultimate sin offering for the world when he was nailed to a Roman cross. Some will tell you the

Jewish people killed Yeshua. They delivered him up to the Romans who conducted the actual execution of the Messiah. But in fact it was God's plan all along. More than 500 years before the Messiah came and died for our sins, Isaiah the Hebrew prophet wrote of God's hand in his future sacrifice stating: "Yet it pleased the Lord to bruise him" Isa 53:10.

The plain fact of the matter is we all had a hand in the death of Yeshua. It was my sin and yours that sent him to the cross. For it was there in the greatest demonstration of love, the whole universe, the worlds seen and invisible, kingdoms of angels, demons and men, were stunned into shocked silence as the son of God himself took upon himself the justified wrath of God, due to us all, in order to offer a way of escape from the future great tribunal of God when all shall stand before him and give an account of our lives.

Sin, rebellion against his law, is punishable by eternal death in the lake of fire. But because he is just and cannot let the guilty go free he came to earth in the form of his son and offered himself in our place so we do not have to face his wrath and the lake of fire.

Incredibly the creator died to save his own rebellious creation.

Our part is to accept that sacrifice as ours, for us; call on God for his forgiveness in light of that sacrifice, turn from our rebellious ways and walk from this day on following and obeying him.

That is Messiah revealed in the ancient Hebrew sacrificial system.

Just 40 years after the crucifixion of Yeshua the Temple in Jerusalem was destroyed by the armies of the Roman General Titus.

Yeshua's sacrifice was the once and for all final sin offering.

For the last 2,000 years no Jew can find forgiveness unless he comes to God through Yeshua and his sacrifice.This is true also for the entire world. No Mass in Roman Catholic Churches can remove sin or take us one millimetre closer to God. Nothing but the one sacrifice, never repeated, will save us. We can get no nearer to God if we refuse to come by way of the one door and the one sacrifice. There are no alternative ways to be forgiven and have a real relationship with the living God. It is through Messiah and him alone we find peace with God.

Now we have come by the door and the sacrifice we are confronted with the Laver of cleansing. This also is a pre-figuration of the coming Messiah Yeshua

(fig 7)

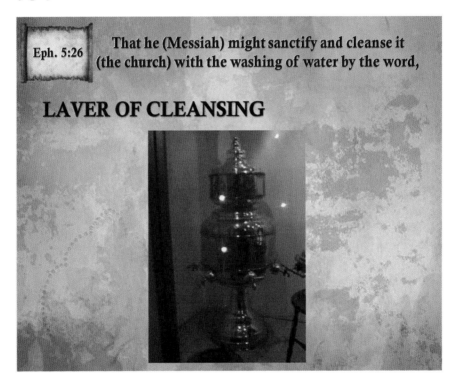

Eph. 5:26   That he (Messiah) might sanctify and cleanse it (the church) with the washing of water by the word,

LAVER OF CLEANSING

The Messiah is known as the word of God. In John chapter 1 verse 1 concerning the Messiah, we read: "In the beginning was the Word, and the Word was with God, and the Word was God."

Cults such as the Jehovah's Witnesses try to tell us the wording should be "the Word was (a) god." But this is not how the Greek reads at all. Also what the Jehovah's Witnesses miss completely is the fact that though they believe Yeshua was created the Greek shows us clearly when the beginning began, the Word (Messiah) was already in existence. He was there before the beginning of creation. Therefore, he could not have been part of creation but must have existed before.

That makes him exactly what John said he was: God!

In the beginning WAS the Word… not "the Word became".

Also being the very Word of God the now risen Messiah leads us and teaches us through the influence of the Holy Spirit (Ruach Ha Kodesh). As we read (him) his word we are cleansed, washed and shown the way in which we should live our lives so we are better placed to be in the presence of God (Ephesians 5:26). Just as the priests needed to be cleaned for service in the Tabernacle so now followers of Messiah who have entered in through him alone and by his sacrifice need to be daily cleaned and prepared for service. This is done through daily communication with him in prayer and through the reading and imbibing of his word, confessing any and every sin that may create a barrier between us.

So now on our journey to find the Messiah in the Hebrew bible we have come to enter the Holy Tabernacle itself.

As we enter we notice at once how the light within is reflected off the golden boards that made up the inner walls of the Tabernacle. This first inner room is known as the Holy place. The light we see is emanating from the golden candlestick, the Menorah, placed on the south side of the Holy place.

We remember the Lord Yeshua said "I am the light of the world. He who follows me shall not walk in darkness but have the light of life" John 8:12. Without the light from the Menorah all who attempt to enter the Holy Place would indeed walk in darkness. All those who believe they can enter the presence of God without Yeshua are in complete spiritual darkness.

(Fig 8)

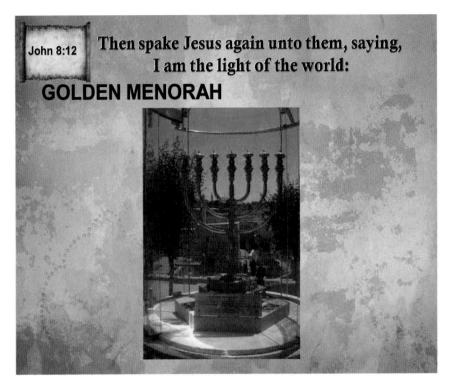

John 8:12 — Then spake Jesus again unto them, saying, I am the light of the world:

GOLDEN MENORAH

Vainly they attempt to enter by some other way other than the one door and the final sacrifice. They do not feel the need of the word to cleanse them and show them the way. Therefore, when they try to find God they enter a black spiritual void because they have disregarded the only one who lights the way to the presence of God.

The result may be spiritual pride and confusion, or realisation they are wrong, from which the only remedy is to retrace their steps to the door and the sacrifice and begin again by the correct, God ordained way.

To the north of the Menorah we find the Table of Shewbread

The 12 loaves, representing the 12 tribes of Israel, were there to be eaten by the priests every week. Messiah said "I am the bread of life" meaning he has no sin in him and we are to look to him for our spiritual

(Fig 9)

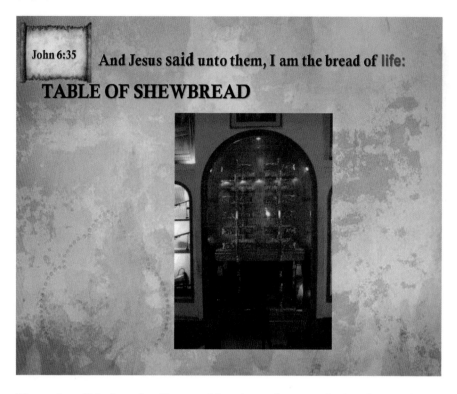

John 6:35   And Jesus said unto them, I am the bread of life:

TABLE OF SHEWBREAD

life and well being, feeding on him through our relationship with him and his word.

What a marvellous privilege it is to walk with Israel's Messiah saviour through the wilderness of this world with all its troubles and problems. Who wouldn't want to know and enjoy him the source of life itself?

Next as we face west we see the curtain that separates us from the most Holy place; the Holy of Holies where the Ark of the Covenant stood.

But our way is barred by one more item; the Altar of Incense. This is where the priest would offer incense and prayers on behalf of the people.

Fig 10)

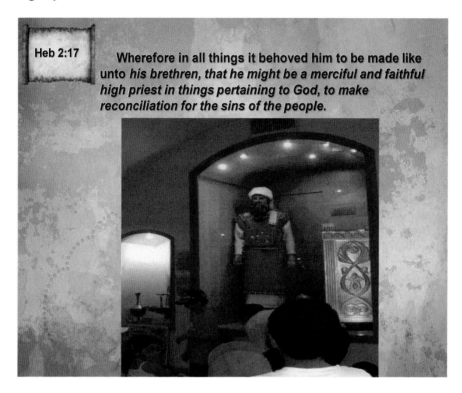

Heb 2:17   Wherefore in all things it behoved him to be made like unto *his brethren, that he might be a merciful and faithful high priest in things pertaining to God, to make reconciliation for the sins of the people.*

As the text above states Yeshua became a high priest to make reconciliation for the sins of the people. Not for the Jewish people alone but for the whole world. The bible also says he daily offers prayers for us. How wonderful to have a high priest who daily intercedes for his own people that have come to him. Do you, dear reader, have someone who intercedes for you? There are friends on earth who say they will pray for us. But oh how far above all friendships is the faithful high priest Yeshua the Messiah who today stands before his father in the heavenly throne room with your name on his lips if you are his.

But how tragic, how terrifying is the state of that person who has no one to represent him in the heavenly court. But on the day of judgement he must stand, covered with his guilt, before an angry God, completely alone and condemned because he chose to ignore the love and sacrifice of the Messiah. His only way to escape judgement is now lost to him forever with no plea for clemency, not the slightest glimmer of hope for forgiveness. Only the dark and yawning chasm leading to the lake of fire awaits him.

Dear friend, turn while there is yet time. Run to Yeshua, for your very eternal well being depends solely on your relationship with him; the door to God, the sacrifice for your sin, the Word of God, the light of the world, the bread of life, the great high priest of his people. The writer of the book of Hebrews says: "How shall we escape if we neglect so great salvation?" Hebrews 2:3.

Indeed, after all God has done to secure your rescue from his judgement, how shall you escape on that day if today you ignore the only avenue open to you?

Now we have entered the final compartment of the Tabernacle: the Holy of Holies where the Ark of the Covenant stands before us. Made of wood and covered with pure gold, its lid created from one piece of pure gold with the two heavenly beings, the Cherubim, standing facing each other with heads and wings lowered toward the Ark itself. In this most holy place the high priest would enter once each year and sprinkle the blood of the sacrifice on the holy object for the forgiveness of the sins of the nation. (Lev. 16:12-17).

Since the death, burial and resurrection of the Messiah Yeshua no other sacrifices for sin have been recognised by God. In the New Testament letter to the Hebrews chapter 9 we read of the Messiah's high priestly office in which he entered once and for all into the heavenly Holy of Holies where he offered his own blood for the redemption of the entire planet.

Of course, many of our Jewish friends cannot see how the Messiah would ever offer his own blood for our redemption. How could he be the son of God, a divine being, God himself in the flesh...and die on a Roman cross for our sins? But he did and in doing so he opened the way into the holiest place for all those are cleansed by his blood.

As Yeshua died the veil of the Temple was torn in two from top to bottom. In the Jewish community even today when one loses a loved one, grief is displayed by the tearing of the garment from the top down. In true Jewish tradition, when his son died for our sins the God of Israel in his great grief tore the curtain of the Temple from the top down, thus opening the way into the holiest place for all who trust in Messiah: enabling us enter the very presence of the God of Israel as his child and priest. What an amazing, merciful God we serve. He makes rebels his own children and calls them into the very closest of relationships with him.

(Fig. 11)

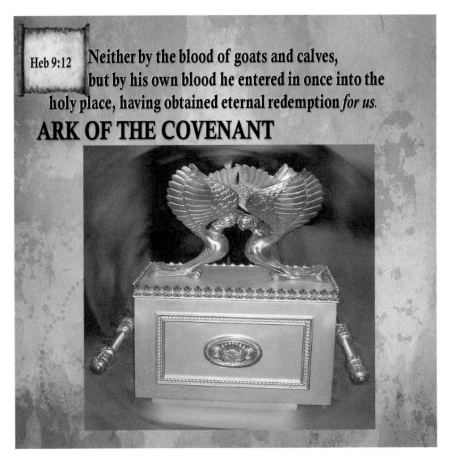

Heb 9:12 Neither by the blood of goats and calves, but by his own blood he entered in once into the holy place, having obtained eternal redemption *for us.*

ARK OF THE COVENANT

Chapter 7

THE CAMP OF ISRAEL AND THE CRUCIFIXION

Yet the very way the tribes camped around the Tabernacle as recorded in the Hebrew Old Testament (Tenach) reveals the amazing truth concerning God's son, the Messiah and his sacrifice. We have seen how every item within the Tabernacle exposes some aspect of the Messiah, the suffering servant of God. But now as the tribes encamped around the Tabernacle itself God's divine hand in the authorship of the scriptures is once more presented to us with astounding clarity.

(Fig. 12)

BENJAMIN: 35,400
MANASSEH: 32,200
EPHRAIM: 40,000
TOTAL: 108,100

GAD: 57,000   NAPHTALI: 53,400
SIMEON: 59,300   ASHER: 41,500
REUBEN: 46,500   DAN: 62,700
TOTAL: 151,450   TOTAL: 157,600

ZEBULUN: 57,400
ISSACHAR: 54,400
JUDAH: 74,600
TOTAL: 186,400

In our illustration above, we see the setting out of the tribes around the Tabernacle as described in the book of Numbers chapter 1. Notice the tribes of Judah, Issachar and Zebulun number 186,400. The tribes of

Ephraim, Manasseh and Benjamin total 108,100. The bottom tribes totalling more than 78,000 over the top group.

The two groups of tribes to the left and right of our illustration are almost the same with a difference of just 6,150.

Do you know what the camp of Israel formed as they camped around the Tabernacle of God?

(Fig 13)

A cross. The symbol of the Messiah Yeshua's sacrifice displayed in the setting out of the tribes of Israel as they camped around the Tabernacle; the items of which all pointed to some aspect of the Messiah's ministry as the One way; the Sacrifice; the Word; the Bread of life; Light of the

31

world; Intercessor for his people and Divine High priest. And around this emblem of Messiah we see, in the setting out of the twelve tribes of Israel, the cross of his sacrifice displayed thousands of years before the punishment of crucifixion was ever invented. How wonderful are the working of the God of Israel. Showing the sacrifice of Messiah thousands of years before he came, written by Jewish scribes, many of whom did not believe Messiah would come and die on a cross. Yet here it is. Who can help but be utterly stunned into awe and worship of the God who loves us so much he left absolutely nothing in his word to chance. Chance is not an option in the workings of God. This is a message from eternity to tell us who the Messiah is and why he came, regardless of the disbelief of those who placed these records before us all those millennia ago. But we must move deeper.

When we look again at the main tribes as they encamped around the Holy Tabernacle we discover yet another evidence of the hand of God in the planning of events to be recorded in the scriptures. If we look at the root meaning behind the Hebrew names of the head tribes as they camped we again are stunned into absolute astonishment as God reveals his son.

(Fig 14)

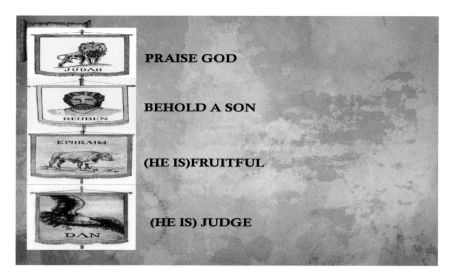

PRAISE GOD

BEHOLD A SON

(HE IS)FRUITFUL

(HE IS) JUDGE

As they camped their banners silently shouted to the universe and beyond the message of the coming Messiah: Praise God, Behold a son, He is fruitful and he is the judge. As they gazed up into the starry heavens above their desert camp the host of heaven looked down and read the message of the ages.

(Fig 15)

Could the creator of all things have made his message any clearer? The Tabernacle and its items speak of Messiah's ministry and person; the tribes create the object of his sacrifice, a cross, as they make camp; the very names of the lead tribes send a message to the starry skies that gaze down on the Tabernacle and the cross; Praise God Behold a son He is fruitful and He is the judge.

How can anyone who really investigates these wonders doubt the existence of a supreme being, God, who rules and reigns and even places his eternal message of redemptive love amongst those whose descendents would read their records and yet could not believe Messiah would die for them. Yet here hidden within the objects, the settings and the names is the gospel of Jesus Christ, Yeshua Ha' Mashiach, Yeshua the Messiah.

Chapter 8

THE MYSTERY OF THE TORAH

The word "Torah" is not a Christian, Western word. It is Hebrew. It means teaching. When interest began to grow concerning the bible code it was discovered that if one takes the first Hebrew letter Tav in the book of Genesis and counts 49 letters, stopping at the 50th letter and so on the word Torah is discovered encoded within the text. The same word was discovered at 50 letter intervals in the next book the book of Exodus. When then they came to the third book, Leviticus, Torah was not found. When Numbers and Deuteronomy were checked Torah was found once more at 50 letter intervals. But the code was reversed.

(Fig 16)

(Fig 17)

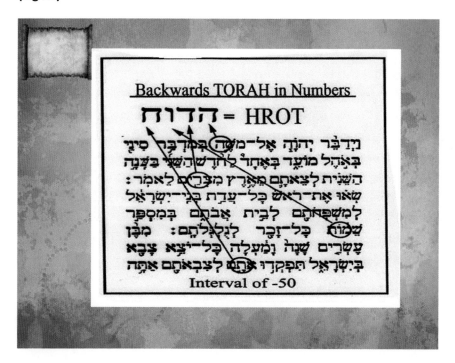

I wondered if there could be anything deeper than just the word Torah that represented the first 5 books of the bible. The word Torah means teaching. Was God trying to teach us something other than that revealed in the surface text of these 5 books?

I went back to my ancient Hebrew Pictographs and began to place the pictures beneath each Hebrew letter to see if there was anything others may have missed. As I placed the relevant pictograph beneath each letter I actually began to cry. The Messiah Code was clear even in the Hebrew word Torah. Reading right to left it reads: On a cross is nailed the highest. Behold.

This is taken from the Hebrew word Torah using ancient Hebrew Pictographs. How can anyone even consider suggesting this is a Christian / Western interpretation of these ancient symbols?

(Fig. 18)

ON A CROSS
IS NAILED
THE HIGHEST
BEHOLD (THIS WONDERFUL SIGHT)

Chapter 9

WHO WAS IT ON THE CROSS?

We have the Hebrew word Torah encoded in Genesis, Exodus, Numbers and Deuteronomy and encoded within is the message "On a cross is nailed the highest. Behold."

In Genesis and Exodus the code is pointing toward the centre book Leviticus and is reversed in the books of Numbers and Deuteronomy.

(Fig 19)

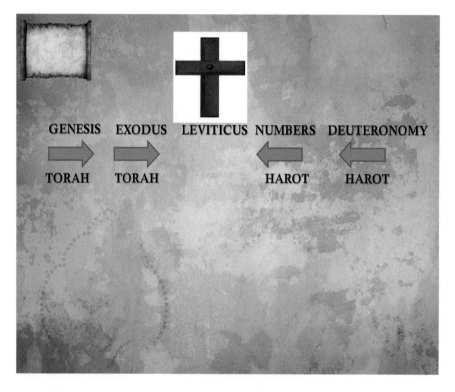

But who is revealed as the one nailed on the cross?

Returning to the centre book Leviticus researchers discovered to their amazement every 7th letter spelled out the divine Hebrew name of God: YHVH.

(Fig 20)

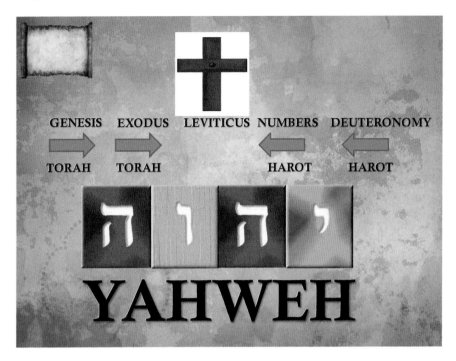

God was on the cross in the form of his son Yeshua. This is inescapable. From Genesis to the very word Torah the Messiah Code reveals the anointed one, the Messiah, who also is God, would come to earth in human form and die on a cross to rescue his own creation from his justice. God has done everything he can to save us from the lake of fire. He is just. To let the guilty go free would make him unjust. So one had to take the punishment in our place. The only one able to do this was one who is pure himself and without sin; God. So we have no excuse on the day we face him and hear our judgement read out against us for our cosmic treason.

Chapter 10

THE MESSAGE HIDDEN IN THE DIVINE NAME

There is just one more revelation for us to consider. It is the divine name of God himself. YHVH.

What do the ancient pictographs reveal encoded within the very name of God? Again as I researched this I felt the tears stinging my eyes.

Reading right to left we read: "The hands behold, the nails behold." Or from left to right " Behold the nails, behold the hands."

(Fig 21)

BEHOLD THE NAILS BEHOLD THE HANDS

God is telling us, in his very name, the story of the Messiah's sacrifice. From eternity the crucifixion of Yeshua has been embedded in the very name of the God of Israel.

What is revealed here is not "Christian". This is revealed in ancient Hebrew names and in the ancient Hebrew pictographs. This is the God of Israel revealing the identity of Israel's and the world's Messiah; the one who died on a cross for their sins. Encoded by a divine hand thousands of years before the event.

I am sure there is much more that can and will be revealed as the world gets ever closer to the Great Day of Judgement when God shall reveal the hearts of all men.

Until that day he is calling to those who will listen "Messiah has come and his name is Yeshua."

Chapter 11

JOSEPH AND YESHUA

One day his ancient people, the Jewish people, will realise the one they rejected is their brother Yeshua.

It is a repeat of the story of Joseph and his brothers.

Joseph was sold to the Gentiles by his brothers.

Jesus was handed to the Gentiles.

Joseph was to all intents and purposes dead and his dreams of greatness he had shared with his family were dead also.

Yeshua is counted as dead and his claims to be Israel's Messiah are looked upon as false and failed.

But when Joseph's brothers became hungry they discovered their brother was not dead but alive and feeding the Gentiles.

In the days ahead Yeshua's brothers, the Jewish people, will cry out for help in their desperate need under Antichrist. But they will discover the one who will come to their rescue is their long thought dead brother, Yeshua. He is alive and has been mostly feeding the Gentiles for the last 2,000 years and how he longs to reveal himself to his people, his brothers, and feed them with forgiveness and eternal life.

In his great love for all men God has placed within his word unfailing evidence that Yeshua is the Messiah; the God man who came to earth with one mission; to receive the wrath of God as he hung on a cross between heaven and earth. He stood in our place between God and us and took the full force of the judgement we deserve.

That is the greatest love story you will ever hear. He loved us even though we were rebels and fully deserved no mercy but his righteous judgement. And he came and lived and died and rose again with one purpose: to save you and me from an eternity in the Lake of Fire.

What love!

How will you respond? Will you put this book to one side and disregard the message contained within its pages? Or will you turn in gratitude and repentance toward the loving God who has done all he can to rescue you from his own court?

Make no mistake regardless of what we say or like to think there is a day coming when all will stand in that court. The date is set in Heaven; you will be there.

My prayer is that you will indeed consider these things, do your own research if you wish. But I pray you will receive this amazing gift God is offering you at this moment; the gift of forgiveness and eternal life and joy with him forever as his child.

The bible says in John chapter 1 verse 12 "To as many as received him (Yeshua / Jesus) to them he gave the power to become the sons of God; even to those who believed on his name."

These words are true and trustworthy.

I pray you make that decision, before it is too late, and become a child of God through the one door, the only sacrifice, the word of God, Light of the world, Bread of life, Our great high priest.

YESHUA HA'MASHIACH / JESUS THE MESSIAH.

May God bless and guide you in your journey.

Please visit our blog at:

http://www.shofar-ministries.blogspot.co.uk

Also visit us on YouTube. Simply search for "Shofar Ministries"

To purchase the 90 minute DVD visit our DVD store:

http://goo.gl/AFZs4D

To contact Bob Mitchell please e-mail:

shofaruk2@yahoo.com

Printed in Great Britain
by Amazon